Editor
Gisela Lee, M.A.

Managing Editor
Karen Goldfluss, M.S. Ed.

Editor-in-Chief
Sharon Coan, M.S. Ed.

Cover Artist
Barb Lorseyedi

Art Manager
Kevin Barnes

Art Director
CJae Froshay

Imaging
Rosa C. See

Product Manager
Phil Garcia

Publisher
Mary D. Smith, M.S. Ed.

Author

Robert Smith

Teacher Created Resources, Inc.
6421 Industry Way
Westminster, CA 92683
www.teachercreated.com

ISBN: 978-0-7439-8626-7

©2004 Teacher Created Resources, Inc.
Reprinted, 2013
Made in U.S.A.

🐚 🐚 🐚 🐚 🐚 Table of Contents 🐚 🐚 🐚 🐚

Introduction

The old adage "practice makes perfect" can really hold true for your child and his or her education. The more practice and exposure your child has with concepts being taught in school, the more success he or she is likely to find. For many parents, knowing how to help your children can be frustrating because the resources may not be readily available. As a parent it is also difficult to know where to focus your efforts so that the extra practice your child receives at home supports what he or she is learning in school.

This book has been designed to help parents and teachers reinforce basic skills with their children. *Practice Makes Perfect* reviews basic math skills for children in grade 6. The math focus is geometry. While it would be impossible to include all concepts taught in grade grade 6 in this book, the following basic objectives are reinforced through practice exercises. These objectives support math standards established on a district, state, or national level. (Refer to the Table of Contents for the specific objectives of each practice page.)

- describing and classifying angles
- identifying congruent and similar figures
- drawing lines of symmetry
- describing triangles
- measuring angles in a triangle

- naming plane and solid geometric figures
- identifying faces, edges, and vertices
- finding perimeter and area of polygons, triangles, circles, etc.
- finding volume of 3-dimensional shapes

There are 36 practice pages organized sequentially, so children can build their knowledge from more basic skills to higher-level math skills. (Note: Have children show all work where computation is necessary to solve a problem. For multiple choice responses on practice pages, children can fill in the letter choice or circle the answer.) Following the practice pages are six practice tests. These provide children with multiple-choice test items to help prepare them for standardized tests administered in schools. As your child completes each test, he or she should fill in the correct bubbles on the answer sheet (page 46). To correct the test pages and the practice pages in this book, use the answer key provided on pages 47 and 48.

How to Make the Most of This Book

Here are some useful ideas for optimizing the practice pages in this book:

- Set aside a specific place in your home to work on the practice pages. Keep it neat and tidy with materials on hand.

- Set up a certain time of day to work on the practice pages. This will establish consistency. An alternative is to look for times in your day or week that are less hectic and conducive to practicing skills.

- Keep all practice sessions with your child positive and constructive. If the mood becomes tense, or you and your child are frustrated, set the book aside and look for another time to practice with your child.

- Help with instructions if necessary. If your child is having difficulty understanding what to do or how to get started, work through the first problem with him or her.

- Review the work your child has done. This serves as reinforcement and provides further practice.

- Allow your child to use whatever writing instruments he or she prefers. For example, colored pencils can add variety and pleasure to drill work.

- Pay attention to the areas in which your child has the most difficulty. Provide extra guidance and exercises in those areas. Allowing children to use drawings and manipulatives, such as coins, tiles, game markers, or flash cards, can help them grasp difficult concepts more easily.

- Look for ways to make real-life applications to the skills being reinforced.

Practice 1

Reminders

- An acute angle measures less than 90°.
- A right angle measures exactly 90°.
- An obtuse angle measures more than 90° and less than 180°.
- A straight angle measures exactly 180°.

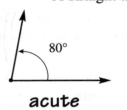 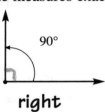 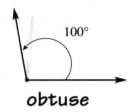 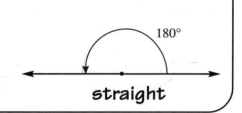

acute   **right**   **obtuse**   **straight**

Directions: Label each of these angles as acute, right, obtuse, or straight angles.

1.

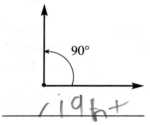

90°

~~right~~ right

2.

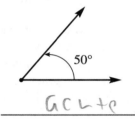

50°

acute

3.

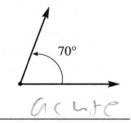

70°

acute

4.

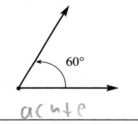

60°

acute

5.

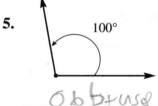

100°

obtuse

6.

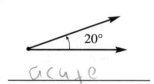

20°

acute

7.

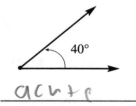

40°

acute

8.

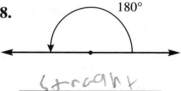

180°

straight

9.

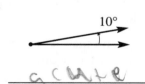

10°

acute

10.

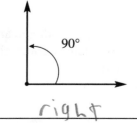

90°

right

11.

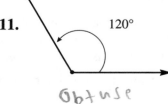

120°

obtuse

12.

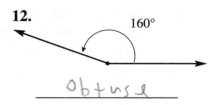

160°

obtuse

Practice 2

Reminders

- An acute angle measures less than 90°.
- A right angle measures exactly 90°.
- An obtuse angle measures more than 90° and less than 180°.
- A straight angle measures exactly 180°.

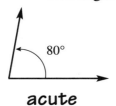
acute

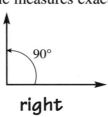
right

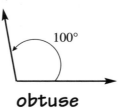
obtuse

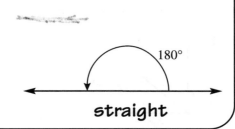
straight

Directions: Label each of these angles as acute, right, obtuse, or straight angles.

1.

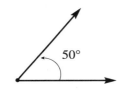
50°

_____

2.

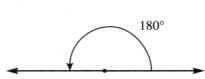
180°

_____

3.

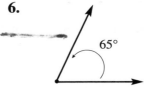
70°

_____

4.

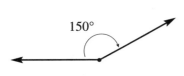
150°

_____

5.

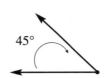
45°

_____

6.

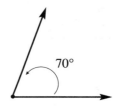
65°

_____

7.

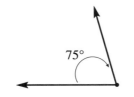
75°

_____

8.

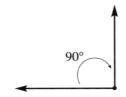
90°

_____

9.

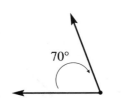
70°

_____

10.

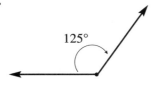
125°

_____

11.

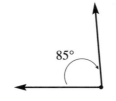
85°

_____

12.

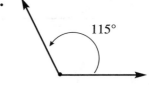
115°

_____

Practice 3

Reminder

- Any two angles whose sum is 90° are complementary.
- Any two angles whose sum is 180° are supplementary.

Directions: Find the complement for each angle shown below.

1. 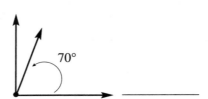 40° _____

2. 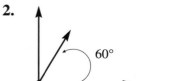 60° _____

3. 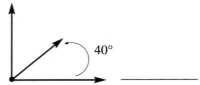 25° _____

4. 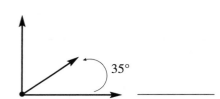 45° _____

5. 70° _____

6. 35° _____

Directions: Find the supplement of each angle shown below.

7.  60° _____

8.  70° _____

9. 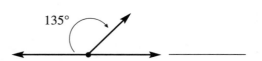 135° _____

10.  90° _____

11.  25° _____

12. 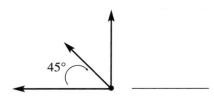 45° _____

13.  75° _____

14.  20° _____

Practice 4

Reminder

- Adjacent angles are next to each other on a transversal.
- Adjacent angles are supplementary.
- Corresponding angles are in the same position on different lines.
- Corresponding angles are congruent. They are the same size.

Directions: Use the graphics to answer each set of questions.

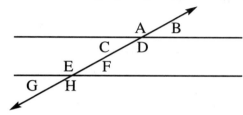

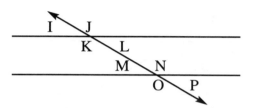

1. Name the eight pairs of adjacent angles.

   Angle _____ and Angle _____

   Angle _____ and Angle _____

   Angle _____ and Angle _____

   Angle _____ and Angle _____

   Angle _____ and Angle _____

   Angle _____ and Angle _____

   Angle _____ and Angle _____

   Angle _____ and Angle _____

2. Name the four pairs of corresponding angles.

   Angle _____ and Angle _____

   Angle _____ and Angle _____

   Angle _____ and Angle _____

   Angle _____ and Angle _____

3. Compute the measurement of each angle.

   Angle A = _____   Angle E = _____

   Angle B = _____   Angle F = _____

   Angle C = _____   Angle G = _____

   Angle D = _____   Angle H = _____

4. Name the eight pairs of adjacent angles.

   Angle _____ and Angle _____

   Angle _____ and Angle _____

   Angle _____ and Angle _____

   Angle _____ and Angle _____

   Angle _____ and Angle _____

   Angle _____ and Angle _____

   Angle _____ and Angle _____

   Angle _____ and Angle _____

5. Name the four pairs of corresponding angles.

   Angle _____ and Angle _____

   Angle _____ and Angle _____

   Angle _____ and Angle _____

   Angle _____ and Angle _____

6. Compute the measurement of each angle.

   Angle I = _____   Angle M = _____

   Angle J = _____   Angle N = _____

   Angle K = _____   Angle O = _____

   Angle L = _____   Angle P = _____

Practice 5

> **Reminder**
> - Vertical angles are formed when two lines intersect.
> - Vertical angles are congruent. They are the same size.
> - Alternate angles are on opposite sides of the transversal.
> - Alternate exterior are congruent. They are the same size.

Directions: Use the transversal in this illustration to answer these questions.

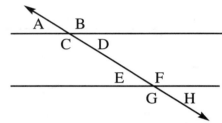 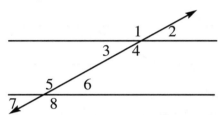

1. Name the four pairs of vertical angles.

   Angle _____ and Angle _____

   Angle _____ and Angle _____

   Angle _____ and Angle _____

   Angle _____ and Angle _____

4. Name the four pairs of vertical angles.

   Angle _____ and Angle _____

   Angle _____ and Angle _____

   Angle _____ and Angle _____

   Angle _____ and Angle _____

2. Name the four pairs of alternate angles.

   Angle _____ and Angle _____

   Angle _____ and Angle _____

   Angle _____ and Angle _____

   Angle _____ and Angle _____

5. Name the four pairs of alternate angles.

   Angle _____ and Angle _____

   Angle _____ and Angle _____

   Angle _____ and Angle _____

   Angle _____ and Angle _____

3. Compute the measurement of each angle.

   Angle A = _____   Angle E = _____

   Angle B = _____   Angle F = _____

   Angle C = _____   Angle G = _____

   Angle D = _____   Angle H = _____

6. Compute the measurement of each angle.

   Angle 1 = _____   Angle 5 = _____

   Angle 2 = _____   Angle 6 = _____

   Angle 3 = _____   Angle 7 = _____

   Angle 4 = _____   Angle 8 = _____

#8626 Practice Makes Perfect: Geometry

Practice 6

Directions: Use a protractor to measure each of the angles below. Write the number of degrees and the name of each angle: acute, right, obtuse, or straight.

1.
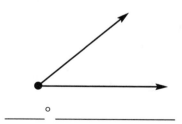
____° _____

2.
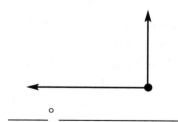
____° _____

3.

____° _____

4.
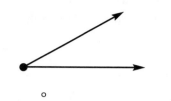
____° _____

5.
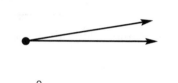
____° _____

6.
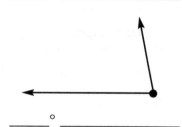
____° _____

7.
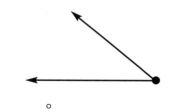
____° _____

8.
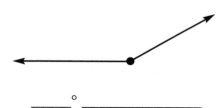
____° _____

9.
____° _____

10.

____° _____

11.
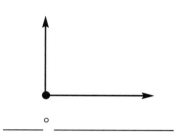
____° _____

12.
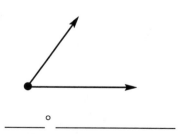
____° _____

Practice 7

Reminders

- A right triangle has one 90° angle.
- An equilateral triangle has three equal sides and three equal angles of 60° each.
- An isosceles triangle has two equal sides and two equal angles.
- A scalene triangle has no equal sides and no equal angles.
- An isosceles right triangle has one 90° angle and two 45° angles. The sides adjacent (next to) the right angle are equal.
- An acute triangle has all three angles less than 90°.
- An obtuse triangle has one angle greater than 90°.
- Triangles can have more than one name.

   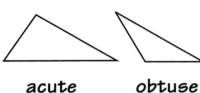

| right | equilateral | isosceles | scalene | acute | obtuse |

Directions: Identify each triangle. If the triangle has more than one name, use both names.

1.

_____

2.

_____

3.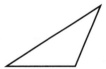

_____

4.

_____

5.

_____

6.

_____

7.

_____

8.

_____

9.

_____

Practice 8

Directions: Compute the number of degrees in each unmarked angle.

1.

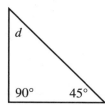

_____

2.

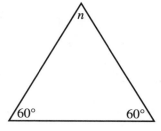

_____

3.

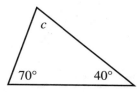

_____

4.

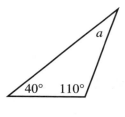

_____

5.

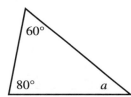

_____

6.

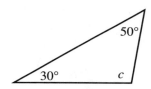

_____

7.

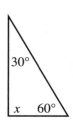

_____

8.

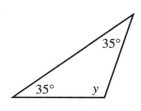

_____

9.

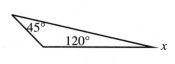

_____

10.

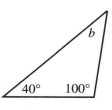

_____

11.

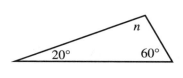

_____

12.

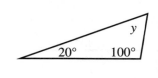

_____

Practice 9

Reminder
- The sum of the interior angles of every triangle is 180°.
- The sum of the exterior angles of any triangle is 360°.

Directions: Compute the number of degrees in each unmarked angle.

1.

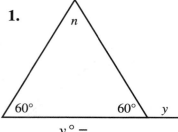

$y° =$ _____

$n° =$ _____

2.

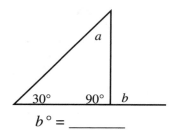

$b° =$ _____

$a° =$ _____

3.

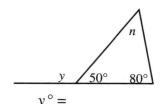

$y° =$ _____

$n° =$ _____

4.

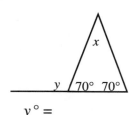

$y° =$ _____

$x° =$ _____

5.

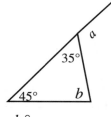

$b° =$ _____

$a° =$ _____

6.

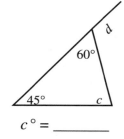

$c° =$ _____

$d° =$ _____

7.

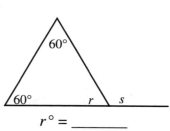

$r° =$ _____

$s° =$ _____

8.

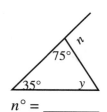

$n° =$ _____

$y° =$ _____

9.

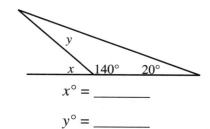

$x° =$ _____

$y° =$ _____

10.

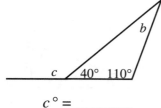

$c° =$ _____

$b° =$ _____

11.

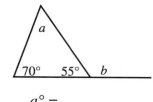

$a° =$ _____

$b° =$ _____

12.

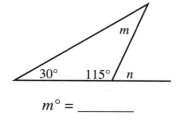

$m° =$ _____

$n° =$ _____

Practice 10

Polygon Names

Triangle

Square

Pentagon

Hexagon

Octagon

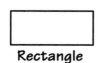
Rectangle

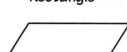
Parallelogram

Rhombus

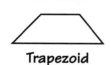
Trapezoid

Directions: Use the names listed on the left to identify each of the polygons below. Use the most specific name for each figure.

1. _____

2. _____

3. _____

4. _____

5. _____

6. _____

7. _____

8. _____

9. _____

10. _____

11. _____

12. _____

Practice 11

> **Reminder**
>
> The interior angles of a quadrilateral always add up to 360°.

Directions: Compute the number of degrees in each unmarked angle.

1.

x = _____

2.

x = _____

3.

x = _____

4.

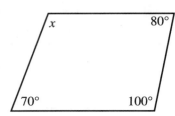

x = _____

5.

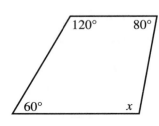

x = _____

6.

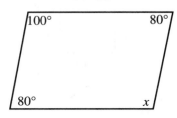

x = _____

7.

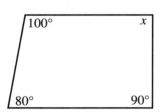

x = _____

8.

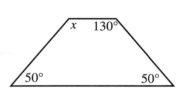

x = _____

9.

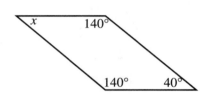

x = _____

10.

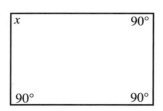

x = _____

11.

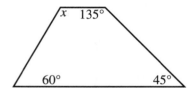

x = _____

12.

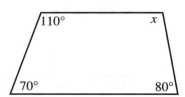

x = _____

Practice 12

Directions: Compute the perimeter of these rectangles.

1.

20 m

12 meters

_____

2.

18 ft.

21 ft.

_____

3.

25 cm

13 cm

_____

4.

45 in.

30 in.

_____

5.

38 yds.

17 yds.

_____

6.

63 mm

19 mm

_____

7.

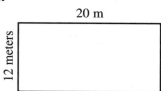

122 cm

49 cm

_____

8.

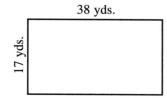

198 mm

36 mm

_____

9.

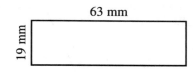

229.4 m

37.1 m

_____

10.

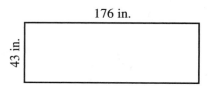

176 in.

43 in.

_____

11.

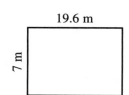

19.6 m

7 m

_____

12.

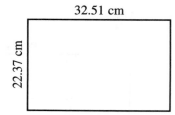

32.51 cm

22.37 cm

_____

Practice 13

Directions: Compute the perimeter of these shapes

1.

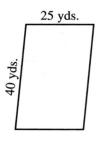

25 yds.

40 yds.

_____

2.

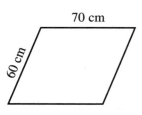

70 cm

60 cm

_____

3.

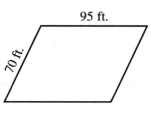

95 ft.

70 ft.

_____

4.

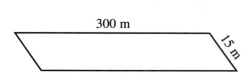

300 m

15 m

_____

5.

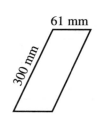

45 cm

80 cm

_____

6.

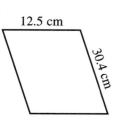

61 mm

300 mm

_____

7.

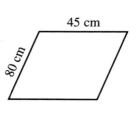

90.2 m

20.3 m

_____

8.

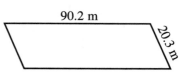

12.5 cm

30.4 cm

_____

Practice 14 ꙮ ꙮ ꙮ ꙮ ꙮ ꙮ ꙮ ꙮ ꙮ ꙮ ꙮ ꙮ ꙮ ꙮ

Reminder

- The perimeter of a regular polygon is computed by multiplying the length of one side by the number of sides.
- The perimeter of a polygon with unequal sides is computed by adding the lengths of each side.

Directions: Compute the perimeter of each polygon.

1.
16 m

_____

2.
25 cm

_____

3.
31 yds.

_____

4.
35 mm

_____

5.
45 in.

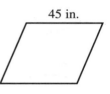

_____

6.
25 mm

_____

7.
15 ft.

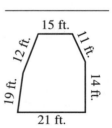

15 ft.

_____

8.
34 cm

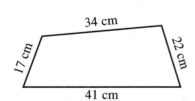

_____

9.
36 m

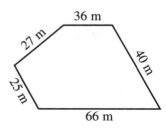

_____

10.
81 mm

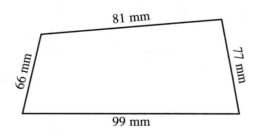

_____

Practice 15

Directions: Compute the circumference of each circle.

1.

10 in.

C = _____

2.

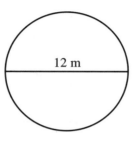

12 m

C = _____

3.

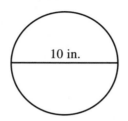

9 in.

C = _____

4.

8 ft.

C = _____

5.

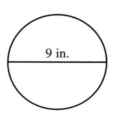

15 cm

C = _____

6.

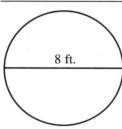

20 m

C = _____

7.

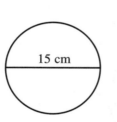

25 ft.

C = _____

8.

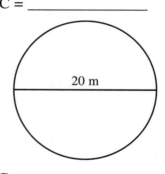 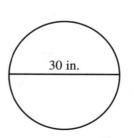 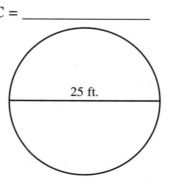

30 in.

C = _____

Practice 16

Reminder

- The circumference is the distance around a circle.
- Pi = 3.14
- The circumference can be computed by multiplying 3.14 times the diameter. **C = πd**
- The circumference can be computed by multiplying 2 times the radius times 3.14. **C = 2 πr**

Directions: Compute the circumference of each circle.

1.

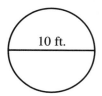

C = _____

2.

C = _____

3.

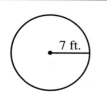

C = _____

4.

C = _____

5.

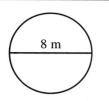

C = _____

6.

C = _____

7.

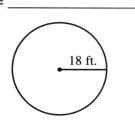

C = _____

8.

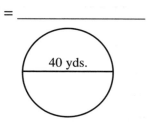

C = _____

9.

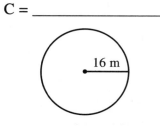

C = _____

10.

C = _____

Practice 17

Reminder

- The area of a flat surface is a measure of how much space is covered by that surface.
- Area is measured in square units.
- The area of a rectangle equals length times width or **A = l x w**

Directions: Compute the number of square cm in these figures.

1. _____cm^2

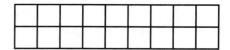

2. _____cm^2

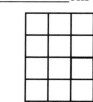

3. _____cm^2

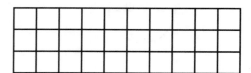

4. _____cm^2

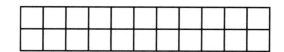

5. _____cm^2

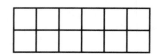

6. _____cm^2

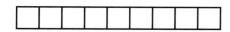

7. _____cm^2

8. _____cm^2

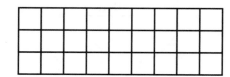

9. _____cm^2

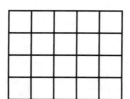

10. _____cm^2

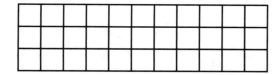

Practice 18

Reminder

- The area of a rectangle is computed by multiplying the width of one side times the length of the adjoining side.
- This may also be expressed as multiplying the base times the height or **A = l x w** or **A = b x h**

Directions: Compute the area of each rectangle.

1.

30 in.

20 in.

_____ in.^{2}

2.

25 m

12 m

_____ m^2

3.

23 cm

18 cm

_____ cm^2

4.

63 mm

47 mm

_____ mm^2

5.

75 ft.

19 ft.

_____ ft.^{2}

6.

81 m

63 m

_____ m^2

7. w = 96 yards
   l = 57 yards
   A = _____

8. w = 76 in.
   l = 29 in.
   A = _____

9. b = 88 m
   h = 67 m
   A = _____

10. b = 77 cm
   h = 47 cm
   A = _____

11. b = 3.7 m
   h = 7.1 m
   A = _____

12. b = 9.7 ft.
   h = 12.3 ft.
   A = _____

13. b = 4.7 in.
   h = 2.1 in.
   A = _____

14. b = 9.12 cm
   h = 4 cm
   A = _____

Practice 19

> **Reminder**
>
> The area of a parallelogram is computed by multiplying the base times the height or $A = b \times h$

Directions: Compute the area of each parallelogram.

1.

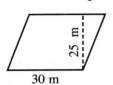

30 m, 25 m

_____ m^2

2.

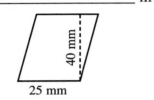

25 mm, 40 mm

_____ mm^2

3.

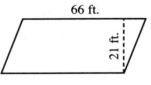

66 ft., 21 ft.

_____ ft.^{2}

4.

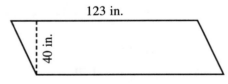

123 in., 40 in.

_____ in.^{2}

5.

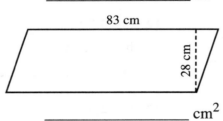

83 cm, 28 cm

_____ cm^2

6.

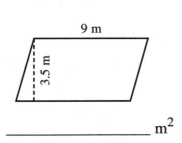

9 m, 3.5 m

_____ m^2

7. b = 56 mm

 h = 41 mm

 A = _____

8. b = 3.1 ft.

 h = 8 ft.

 A = _____

9. b = 300 in.

 h = 48 in.

 A = _____

10. b = 1.9 m

 h = 20 m

 A = _____

11. b = 121 mm

 h = 40 mm

 A = _____

12. b = 7.5 in.

 h = 3.1 in.

 A = _____

13. b = 6.2 m

 h = 3.2 m

 A = _____

14. b = 900 cm

 h = 68 cm

 A = _____

Practice 20

Directions: Compute the area of each parallelogram.

1.
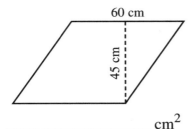
_____ cm^2

2.
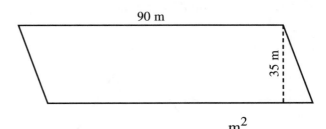
_____ m^2

3.
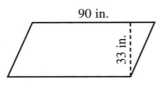
_____ in.^{2}

4.
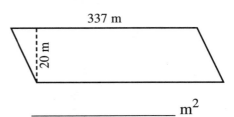
_____ m^2

5.
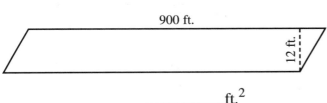
_____ ft.^{2}

6.
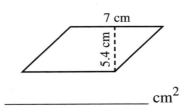
_____ cm^2

7. b = 400 ft.
   h = 300 ft.
   A = _____

8. b = 4.9 m
   h = 2.1 m
   A = _____

9. b = 902 cm
   h = 99 cm
   A = _____

10. b = 9.6 in.
    h = 4.6 in.
    A = _____

11. b = 88.2 m
    h = 50 m
    A = _____

12. b = 934 mm
    h = 300 mm
    A = _____

13. b = 890 in.
    h = 400 in.
    A = _____

14. b = 404 m
    h = 221 m
    A = _____

Practice 21

Reminder

- The area of a triangle is one-half the area of a parallelogram or a rectangle.
- To compute the area of a triangle, multiply the base times the height and divide by 2 or multiply 1/2 the base times the height or **A = 1/2 (b x h)**

Directions: Compute the area of each triangle.

1.

12 in.
20 in.

_____ in.^{2}

2.

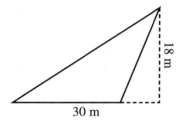

18 m
30 m

_____ m^2

3.

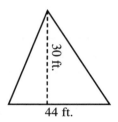

30 ft.
44 ft.

_____ ft.^{2}

4.

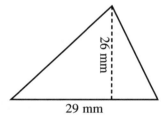

26 mm
29 mm

_____ mm^2

5.

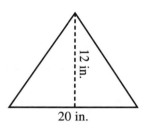

47 cm
50 cm

_____ cm^2

6.

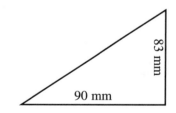

83 mm
90 mm

_____ mm^2

7.

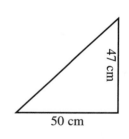

33 in.
69 in.

_____ in.^{2}

8.

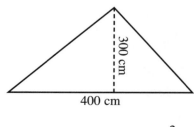

300 cm
400 cm

_____ cm^2

 #8626 Practice Makes Perfect: Geometry

Practice 22 🌀 🐚 🌀 🐚 🌀 🐚 🌀 🐚 🌀 🐚 🌀 🌀 🐚

Directions: Compute the area of each triangle.

1.

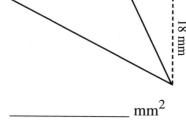

_____ mm^2

2.

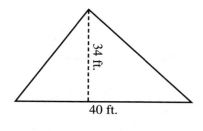

_____ ft.^{2}

3.

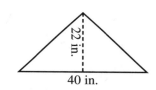

_____ in.^{2}

4.

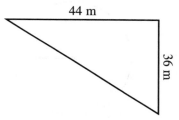

_____ m^2

5.

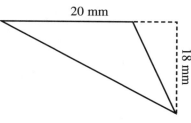

_____ cm^2

6.

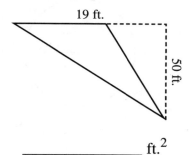

_____ ft.^{2}

7.

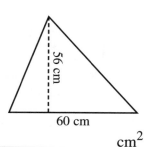

_____ yards^2

8.

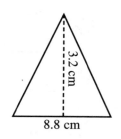

_____ cm^2

Practice 23

Reminder

- The area of a circle is computed by multiplying the radius times itself and that answer by 3.14.
- $A = \pi r^2$ (Pi times the radius squared) (Remember, Pi = 3.14)

Directions: Compute the area of each circle.

1.

A = _____ in.^{2}

2.

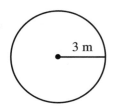

A = _____ m^2

3.

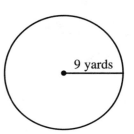

A = _____ yards^2

4.

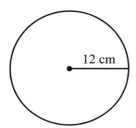

A = _____ cm^2

5.

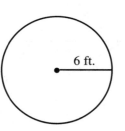

A = _____ ft.^{2}

6.

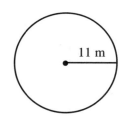

A = _____ m^2

7.

A = _____ in.^{2}

8.

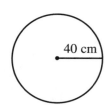

A = _____ cm^2

Practice 24

Reminder

- The area of a circle is computed by multiplying the radius times itself and that answer by 3.14.
- $A = \pi r^2$ (Pi times the radius squared) (Remember, Pi = 3.14)

Directions: Compute the area of each circle.

1.

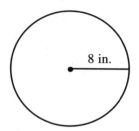

A = _____ in.^{2}

2.

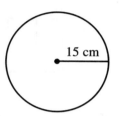

A = _____ cm^2

3.

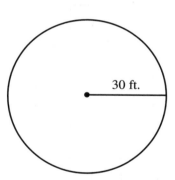

A = _____ ft.^{2}

4.

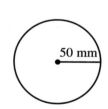

A = _____ mm^2

5.

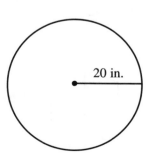

A = _____ in.^{2}

6.

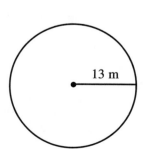

A = _____ m^2

Practice 25

Directions: Compute the volume of each cube.

1.

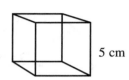

5 cm

V = _____ cm^3

2.

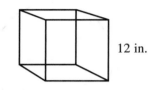

12 in.

V = _____ in.^{3}

3.

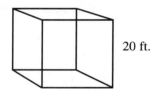

20 ft.

V = _____ ft.^{3}

4.

9 mm

V = _____ mm^3

5.

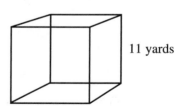

11 yards

V = _____ yards^3

6.

10 cm

V = _____ cm^3

7.

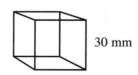

30 mm

V = _____ mm^3

8.

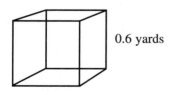

0.6 yards

V = _____ yards^3

Practice 26

Reminder

The volume of a rectangular prism is computed by multiplying the length times the width times the height of the prism or **V = l x w x h** or **V = lwh**

Directions: Compute the volume of each rectangular prism.

1.

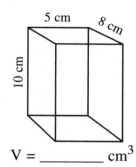

V = _____ cm^3

2.

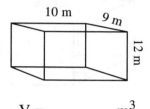

V = _____ m^3

3.

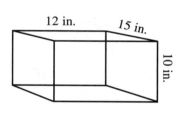

V = _____ in.^{3}

4.

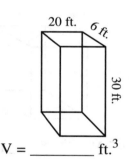

V = _____ ft.^{3}

5.

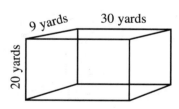

V = _____ yards^3

6.

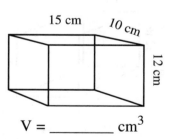

V = _____ cm^3

7.

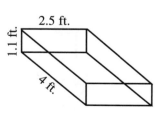

V = _____ ft.^{3}

8.

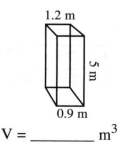

V = _____ m^3

Practice 27

Reminder

The volume of a rectangular prism is computed by multiplying the length times the width times the height of the prism or **V = l x w x h or V = lwh**

Directions: Compute the volume of each rectangular prism

1.

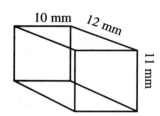

V = _____ mm^3

2.

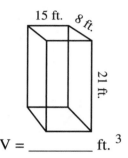

V = _____ ft.^{3}

3.

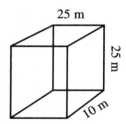

V = _____ m^3

4.

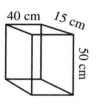

V = _____ cm^3

5.

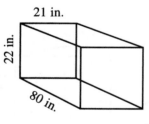

V = _____ in.^{3}

6.

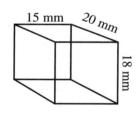

V = _____ mm^3

7.

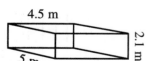

V = _____ m^3

8.

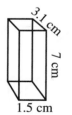

V = _____ cm^3

Practice 28 ꙮ ꙮ ꙮ ꙮ ꙮ ꙮ ꙮ ꙮ ꙮ ꙮ ꙮ ꙮ ꙮ

Reminder

- The volume of a pyramid is 1/3 the volume of a prism with the same base.
- The volume of a pyramid is computed by multiplying 1/3 times the length times the width of the base times the height of the pyramid.

V = 1/3 x l x w x h or V = 1/3 (lwh)

Directions: Compute the volume of each pyramid.

1.

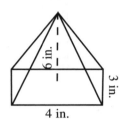

6 in.   3 in.

4 in.

V = _____ in.³

2.

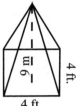

6 in   4 ft.

4 ft.

V = _____ ft.³

3.

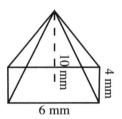

10 mm   4 mm

6 mm

V = _____ mm³

4.

3 in.   5 in.

8 in.

V = _____ in.³

5.

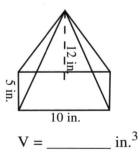

12 in.

5 in.

10 in.

V = _____ in.³

6.

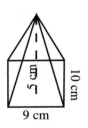

5 cm   10 cm

9 cm

V = _____ cm³

7.

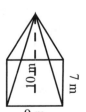

10 m   7 m

9 m

V = _____ m³

8.

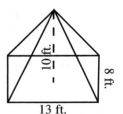

10 ft   8 ft.

13 ft.

V = _____ ft.³

Practice 29

> **Reminder**
>
> The volume of a cylinder is computed by multiplying the height times the area of the base.
>
> $$V = h \times \pi r^2$$

Directions: Compute the volume of each cylinder.

1.

5 cm

7 cm

V = _____ cm^3

2.

4 in.

10 in.

V = _____ in.^{3}

3.

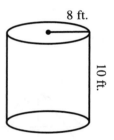

8 ft.

10 ft.

V = _____ ft.^{3}

4.

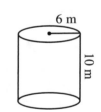

18 cm

10 cm

V = _____ cm^3

5.

8 in.

6 in.

V = _____ in.^{3}

6.

6 m

10 m

V = _____ m^3

7.

7 mm

11 mm

V = _____ mm^3

8.

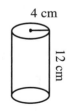

4 cm

12 cm

V = _____ cm^3

Practice 30

Directions: Compute the surface area of each rectangular prism.

1.

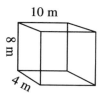

face 1 _____

face 2 _____

face 3 _____

face 4 _____

face 5 _____

face 6 _____

total _____ m^2

2.

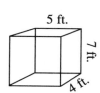

face 1 _____

face 2 _____

face 3 _____

face 4 _____

face 5 _____

face 6 _____

total _____ ft.^{2}

3.

face 1 _____

face 2 _____

face 3 _____

face 4 _____

face 5 _____

face 6 _____

total _____ cm^2

4.

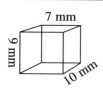

face 1 _____

face 2 _____

face 3 _____

face 4 _____

face 5 _____

face 6 _____

total _____ mm^2

5.

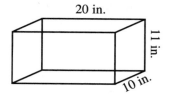

face 1 _____

face 2 _____

face 3 _____

face 4 _____

face 5 _____

face 6 _____

total _____ in.^{2}

6.

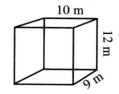

face 1 _____

face 2 _____

face 3 _____

face 4 _____

face 5 _____

face 6 _____

total _____ m^2

Practice 31

Reminder

- A line of symmetry is a line drawn through the center of a flat shape so that one half of the shape can be folded to fit exactly over the other half.
- A figure may have one line of symmetry, several lines of symmetry, or no lines of symmetry.

Directions: Draw one line of symmetry through the symmetrical figures below. Circle the figures which have no line of symmetry.

1.
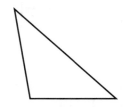

2.
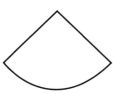

3.
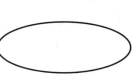

4.
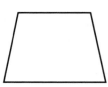

5.

6.
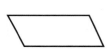

Directions: Draw two or more lines of symmetry through the figures below.

7.

8.

9.
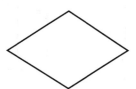

10.
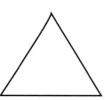

11.

12.

Practice 32

Reminder

Rotational symmetry occurs with a shape that can be rotated around a central point and fitted exactly over itself at a place other than its original position.

Directions: Circle the shapes below which express rotational symmetry. Cross out the figures which do not.

1.

2.

3.

4.

5.

6.

7.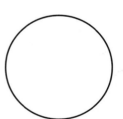

8.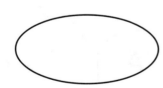

9.

10.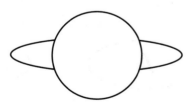

11.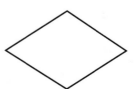

12.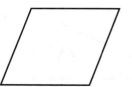

Practice 33

Reminder

- Congruent figures fit exactly over each other.
- Congruent figures are exactly the same in shape and size.
- Congruent figures can be turned over or around to fit.

Directions: Determine which of the figures in each set are congruent. Circle the letters of the congruent figures.

1.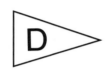

2.

3.

4.

5.

6.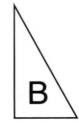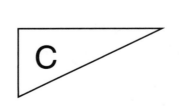

Practice 34

Reminder
- Congruent figures are exactly the same in shape and size.
- Congruent figures can be turned over or around to fit.
- Similar figures are the same in shape but different in size.

Directions: Determine which of the figures in each set are similar and which are congruent.

 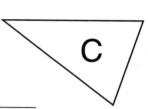 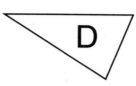

1. Similar _____ Congruent _____

2. Similar _____ Congruent _____

3. Similar _____ Congruent _____

4. Similar _____ Congruent _____

5. Similar _____ Congruent _____

6. Similar _____ Congruent _____

Practice 35

Directions: Identify each of these figures.

1.

   _____

2.

   _____

3.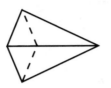

   _____

4.

   _____

5.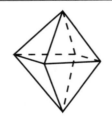

   _____

6.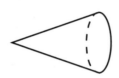

   _____

7.

   _____

8.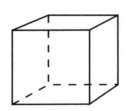

   _____

9.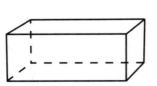

   _____

10.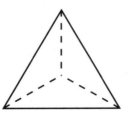

    _____

11.

    _____

12.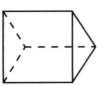

    _____

Practice 36 ᗡ ᗣ ᗡ ᗣ ᗡ ᗣ ᗡ ᗣ ᗡ ᗣ ᗡ ᗣ ᗡ ᗡ ᗣ

> **Reminder**
> - A face is the flat surface of a three dimensional figure.
> - An edge is a line segment where two faces meet.
> - A vertex is the point where edges meet.

Directions: Name each solid. Count the number of faces, edges, and vertices for each geometric solid on this page.

1.
name _____
faces _____
edges _____
vertices _____

2.
name _____
faces _____
edges _____
vertices _____

3.
name _____
faces _____
edges _____
vertices _____

4.
name _____
faces _____
edges _____
vertices _____

5.
name _____
faces _____
edges _____
vertices _____

6.
name _____
faces _____
edges _____
vertices _____

7.
name _____
faces _____
edges _____
vertices _____

8.
name _____
faces _____
edges _____
vertices _____

Test Practice 1 ༄ ༄ ༄ ༄ ༄ ༄ ༄ ༄ ༄ ༄

Directions: Identify each angle or shape. Use the most precise name. On the Answer Sheet, fill in the answer circle for your choice.

1.
- (A) acute
- (B) right
- (C) obtuse
- (D) straight

8.
- (A) scalene
- (B) equilateral
- (C) right
- (D) isosceles

2.
- (A) right
- (B) obtuse
- (C) straight
- (D) right

9.
- (A) right
- (B) obtuse
- (C) scalene
- (D) equilateral

3.
- (A) right
- (B) obtuse
- (C) acute
- (D) straight

10.
- (A) scalene
- (B) equilateral
- (C) right
- (D) isosceles

4.
- (A) acute
- (B) obtuse
- (C) right
- (D) straight

11.
- (A) square
- (B) pentagon
- (C) hexagon
- (D) octagon

5.
- (A) acute
- (B) straight
- (C) obtuse
- (D) right

12.
- (A) hexagon
- (B) trapezoid
- (C) octagon
- (D) parallelogram

6.
- (A) acute
- (B) obtuse
- (C) straight
- (D) right

13.
- (A) rectangle
- (B) pentagon
- (C) octagon
- (D) hexagon

7.
- (A) scalene
- (B) isosceles
- (C) right
- (D) equilateral

14.
- (A) rhombus
- (B) trapezoid
- (C) hexagon
- (D) pentagon

Test Practice 2

Directions: Compute the missing angle in each figure. On the Answer Sheet, fill in the answer circle for your choice.

1.
- Ⓐ 60°
- Ⓑ 120°
- Ⓒ 50°
- Ⓓ 70°

2.
- Ⓐ 90°
- Ⓑ 110°
- Ⓒ 80°
- Ⓓ 270°

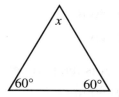

3.
- Ⓐ 90°
- Ⓑ 80°
- Ⓒ 70°
- Ⓓ 120°

4.
- Ⓐ 25°
- Ⓑ 35°
- Ⓒ 50°
- Ⓓ 125°

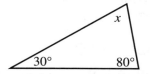

5.
- Ⓐ 90°
- Ⓑ 135°
- Ⓒ 40°
- Ⓓ 60°

6.
- Ⓐ 90°
- Ⓑ 70°
- Ⓒ 80°
- Ⓓ 270°

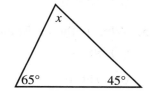

7.
- Ⓐ 90°
- Ⓑ 60°
- Ⓒ 70°
- Ⓓ 120°

8.
- Ⓐ 40°
- Ⓑ 35°
- Ⓒ 70°
- Ⓓ 90°

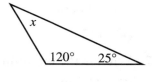

9.
- Ⓐ 50°
- Ⓑ 130°
- Ⓒ 30°
- Ⓓ 90°

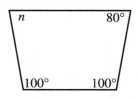

10.
- Ⓐ 60°
- Ⓑ 170°
- Ⓒ 40°
- Ⓓ 50°

11.
- Ⓐ 60°
- Ⓑ 70°
- Ⓒ 80°
- Ⓓ 50°

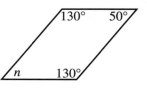

12.
- Ⓐ 70°
- Ⓑ 40°
- Ⓒ 50°
- Ⓓ 120°

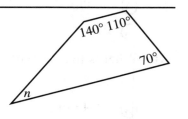

Test Practice 3 🐚 🐚 🐚 🐚 🐚 🐚 🐚 🐚

Directions: Answer each question. On the Answer Sheet, fill in the answer circle for your choice.

1. What is the perimeter of square M?
   - (A) 50 ft.
   - (B) 80 ft.
   - (C) 100 ft.
   - (D) 250 ft.

2. What is the perimeter of rectangle N?
   - (A) 86 in.
   - (B) 88 in.
   - (C) 172 in.
   - (D) 1,833 in.

3. What is the perimeter of rectangle P?
   - (A) 16 cm
   - (B) 332 cm
   - (C) 166 cm
   - (D) 342 cm

4. What is the perimeter of parallelogram R?
   - (A) 133 m
   - (B) 143 m
   - (C) 266 m
   - (D) 286 m

5. What is the perimeter of a rhombus with 44 ft. long sides?
   - (A) 88 ft.
   - (B) 166 ft.
   - (C) 176 ft.
   - (D) 276 ft.

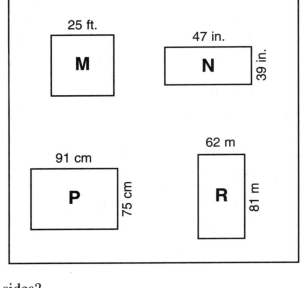

6. What is the perimeter of pentagon S?
   - (A) 195 cm
   - (B) 117 cm
   - (C) 149 cm
   - (D) 234 cm

7. What is the circumference of circle T? (Pi = 3.14)
   - (A) 94.2 in.
   - (B) 78.5 in.
   - (C) 33.4 in.
   - (D) 16.5 in.

8. What is the circumference of circle U? (Pi = 3.14)
   - (A) 62.9 cm
   - (B) 31.4 cm
   - (C) 38.5 cm
   - (D) 314 cm

9. What is the circumference of circle V? (Pi = 3.14)
   - (A) 38 cm
   - (B) 37 cm
   - (C) 376.8 cm
   - (D) 37.68 cm

10. What is the circumference of circle with a diameter of 20 centimeters?
    - (A) 62.8 cm
    - (B) 31.4 cm
    - (C) 61.8 cm
    - (D) 628 cm

Test Practice 4 ଚ ❧ ଚ ❧ ଚ ଚ ❧ ଚ

Directions: Answer each question. On the Answer Sheet, fill in the answer circle for your choice.

1. What is the area of square E?
   - Ⓐ 60 ft.^{2}
   - Ⓒ 120 ft.^{2}
   - Ⓑ 900 ft.^{2}
   - Ⓓ 800 ft.^{2}

2. What is the area of rectangle F?
   - Ⓐ 400 ft.^{2}
   - Ⓒ 45 ft.^{2}
   - Ⓑ 450 ft.^{2}
   - Ⓓ 500 ft.^{2}

3. What is the area of parallelogram G?
   - Ⓐ 28 cm^2
   - Ⓒ 192 cm^2
   - Ⓑ 182 cm^2
   - Ⓓ 56 cm^2

4. What is the area of triangle H?
   - Ⓐ 54 mm^2
   - Ⓒ 540 mm^2
   - Ⓑ 270 mm^2
   - Ⓓ 27 mm^2

5. What is the area of a square with 33 ft. long sides?
   - Ⓐ 66 ft.^{2}
   - Ⓒ 132 ft.^{2}
   - Ⓑ 1,099 ft.^{2}
   - Ⓓ 1,089 ft.^{2}

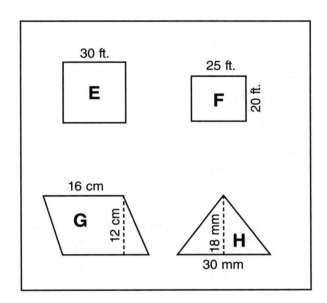

6. What is the area of triangle J?
   - Ⓐ 228 cm^2
   - Ⓒ 218 cm^2
   - Ⓑ 128 cm^2
   - Ⓓ 456 cm^2

7. What is the area of triangle K?
   - Ⓐ 54 in.^{2}
   - Ⓒ 680 in.^{2}
   - Ⓑ 240 in.^{2}
   - Ⓓ 340 in.^{2}

8. What is the area of circle L? (Pi = 3.14)
   - Ⓐ 452.16 mm^2
   - Ⓒ 37.68 mm^2
   - Ⓑ 449.28 mm^2
   - Ⓓ 75.32 mm^2

9. What is the area of circle M? (Pi = 3.14)
   - Ⓐ 1,200 cm^2
   - Ⓒ 1,256 cm^2
   - Ⓑ 1,266 cm^2
   - Ⓓ 62.8 cm^2

10. What is the area of a circle with a 14-inch radius?
   - Ⓐ 615.54 in.^{2}
   - Ⓒ 43.96 in.^{2}
   - Ⓑ 665.44 in.^{2}
   - Ⓓ 615.44 in.^{2}

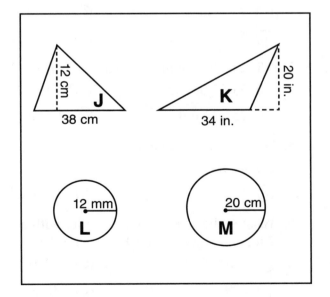

Test Practice 5 🐚 🐚 🐚 🐚 🐚 🐚 🐚 🐚

Directions: Answer each question. On the Answer Sheet, fill in the answer circle for your choice.

1. What is the volume of cube E?
   - Ⓐ 225 in.³
   - Ⓒ 3,235 in.³
   - Ⓑ 3,375 in.³
   - Ⓓ 3,325 in.³

2. What is the volume of prism F?
   - Ⓐ 112 cm³
   - Ⓒ 1,120 cm³
   - Ⓑ 1,020 cm³
   - Ⓓ 32 cm³

3. What is the volume of prism G?
   - Ⓐ 2,220 mm³
   - Ⓒ 48 mm³
   - Ⓑ 2,150 mm³
   - Ⓓ 2,250 mm³

4. What is the volume of a cube 40 ft. on each edge?
   - Ⓐ 6,400 ft.³
   - Ⓒ 64,000 ft.³
   - Ⓑ 120 ft.³
   - Ⓓ 20,000 ft.³

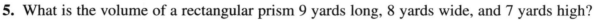

5. What is the volume of a rectangular prism 9 yards long, 8 yards wide, and 7 yards high?
   - Ⓐ 540 yards³
   - Ⓒ 504 yards³
   - Ⓑ 79 yards³
   - Ⓓ 450 yards³

6. What is the volume of cylinder H? (Pi = 3.14)
   - Ⓐ 785 cm³
   - Ⓒ 7,850 cm³
   - Ⓑ 78.5 cm³
   - Ⓓ 7.85 cm³

7. What is the volume of cylinder I? (Pi = 3.14)
   - Ⓐ 3,052.08 mm³
   - Ⓒ 3,152.28 mm³
   - Ⓑ 254.34 mm³
   - Ⓓ 108 mm³

8. What is the volume of pyramid J?
   - Ⓐ 48 cm³
   - Ⓒ 51 cm³
   - Ⓑ 144 cm³
   - Ⓓ 244 cm³

9. What is the volume of a cylinder with a radius of 8 in. and a height of 10 in.? (Pi = 3.14)
   - Ⓐ 2,109.6 in.³
   - Ⓒ 2,009.6 in.³
   - Ⓑ 209.6 in.³
   - Ⓓ 80 in.³

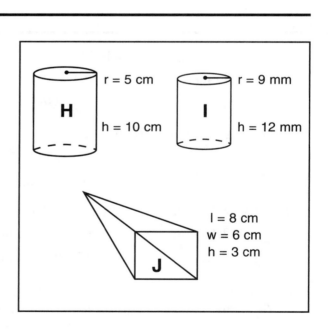

10. What is the volume of a pyramid with a length of 12 ft., a width of 8 ft., and a height of 10 ft.?
    - Ⓐ 330 ft.³
    - Ⓒ 960 ft.³
    - Ⓑ 320 ft.³
    - Ⓓ 3,200 ft.³

Test Practice 6

Directions: Answer each question. On the Answer Sheet, fill in the answer circle for your choice.

1. Which figures are congruent?

ⓐ W and X   ⓑ W and Y   ⓒ Y and Z   ⓓ X and Y

2. Which figures are similar?

ⓐ W, Y, and X   ⓑ X and Y   ⓒ W and Z   ⓓ X and Z

---

3. On which figure can you draw only 5 lines of symmetry?

ⓐ L   ⓑ M   ⓒ O   ⓓ N

4. On which figure can you draw only 3 lines of symmetry?

ⓐ M   ⓑ N   ⓒ O   ⓓ L

5. On which figure can you draw only 1 line of symmetry?

ⓐ L   ⓑ M   ⓒ N   ⓓ O

6. On which figure can you draw only 4 lines of symmetry?

ⓐ L   ⓑ M   ⓒ N   ⓓ O

---

7. Which figure is an octahedron?

ⓐ P   ⓑ Q   ⓒ R   ⓓ S

8. Which figure is a cyclinder?

ⓐ P   ⓑ Q   ⓒ R   ⓓ S

9. Which figure is a rectangular pyramid?

ⓐ P   ⓑ Q   ⓒ R   ⓓ S

10. Which figure is a rectangular prism?

ⓐ P   ⓑ Q   ⓒ R   ⓓ S

Answer Sheet

Test Practice 1

1. (A) (B) (C) (D)
2. (A) (B) (C) (D)
3. (A) (B) (C) (D)
4. (A) (B) (C) (D)
5. (A) (B) (C) (D)
6. (A) (B) (C) (D)
7. (A) (B) (C) (D)
8. (A) (B) (C) (D)
9. (A) (B) (C) (D)
10. (A) (B) (C) (D)
11. (A) (B) (C) (D)
12. (A) (B) (C) (D)
13. (A) (B) (C) (D)
14. (A) (B) (C) (D)

Test Practice 2

1. (A) (B) (C) (D)
2. (A) (B) (C) (D)
3. (A) (B) (C) (D)
4. (A) (B) (C) (D)
5. (A) (B) (C) (D)
6. (A) (B) (C) (D)
7. (A) (B) (C) (D)
8. (A) (B) (C) (D)
9. (A) (B) (C) (D)
10. (A) (B) (C) (D)
11. (A) (B) (C) (D)
12. (A) (B) (C) (D)

Test Practice 3

1. (A) (B) (C) (D)
2. (A) (B) (C) (D)
3. (A) (B) (C) (D)
4. (A) (B) (C) (D)
5. (A) (B) (C) (D)
6. (A) (B) (C) (D)
7. (A) (B) (C) (D)
8. (A) (B) (C) (D)
9. (A) (B) (C) (D)
10. (A) (B) (C) (D)

Test Practice 4

1. (A) (B) (C) (D)
2. (A) (B) (C) (D)
3. (A) (B) (C) (D)
4. (A) (B) (C) (D)
5. (A) (B) (C) (D)
6. (A) (B) (C) (D)
7. (A) (B) (C) (D)
8. (A) (B) (C) (D)
9. (A) (B) (C) (D)
10. (A) (B) (C) (D)

Test Practice 5

1. (A) (B) (C) (D)
2. (A) (B) (C) (D)
3. (A) (B) (C) (D)
4. (A) (B) (C) (D)
5. (A) (B) (C) (D)
6. (A) (B) (C) (D)
7. (A) (B) (C) (D)
8. (A) (B) (C) (D)
9. (A) (B) (C) (D)
10. (A) (B) (C) (D)

Test Practice 6

1. (A) (B) (C) (D)
2. (A) (B) (C) (D)
3. (A) (B) (C) (D)
4. (A) (B) (C) (D)
5. (A) (B) (C) (D)
6. (A) (B) (C) (D)
7. (A) (B) (C) (D)
8. (A) (B) (C) (D)
9. (A) (B) (C) (D)
10. (A) (B) (C) (D)

Answer Key

Page 4
1. right
2. acute
3. acute
4. acute
5. obtuse
6. acute
7. acute
8. straight
9. acute
10. right
11. obtuse
12. obtuse

Page 5
1. acute
2. straight
3. acute
4. obtuse
5. acute
6. acute
7. acute
8. right
9. acute
10. obtuse
11. acute
12. obtuse

Page 6
1. 50°
2. 30°
3. 65°
4. 45°
5. 20°
6. 55°
7. 120°
8. 110°
9. 45°
10. 90°
11. 155°
12. 135°
13. 105°
14. 160°

Page 7
1. A and B
   C and D
   E and F
   G and H
   A and C
   B and D
   E and G
   F and H
2. B and F
   D and H
   A and E
   C and G
3. A = 150°
   B = 30°
   C = 30°
   D = 150°
   E = 150°
   F = 30°
   G = 30°
   H = 150°
4. I and J
   K and L
   M and N
   O and P
   J and L
   N and P
   I and K
   M and O
5. J and N
   L and P
   I and M
   K and O
6. I = 30°
   J = 150°
   K = 150°
   L = 30°

M = 30°
N = 150°
O = 150°
P = 30°

Page 8
1. A and D
   B and C
   E and H
   F and G
2. D and E
   C and F
   B and G
   A and H
3. A = 30°
   B = 150°
   C = 150°
   D = 30°
   E = 30°
   F = 150°
   G = 150°
   H = 30°
4. 1 and 4
   3 and 2
   5 and 8
   6 and 7
5. 3 and 6
   5 and 4
   1 and 8
   2 and 7
6. 1 = 150°
   2 = 30°
   3 = 30°
   4 = 150°
   5 = 150°
   6 = 30°
   7 = 30°
   8 = 150°

Page 9
1. 40° acute
2. 90° right
3. 180° straight
4. 30° acute
5. 10° acute
6. 80° acute
7. 40° acute
8. 150° obtuse
9. 90° right
10. 170° obtuse
11. 15° acute
12. 55° acute

Page 10
1. equilateral
2. right
3. isosceles/obtuse
4. isosceles/right
5. isosceles/obtuse
6. scalene/obtuse
7. isosceles/acute
8. scalene/obtuse

9. isosceles/acute

Page 11
1. d = 45°
2. n = 60°
3. c = 70°
4. a = 30°
5. a = 40°
6. c = 100°
7. x = 90°
8. y = 110°
9. x = 15°
10. b = 40°
11. n = 100°
12. y = 60°

Page 12
1. n = 60°
   y = 120°
2. a = 60°
   b = 90°
3. n = 50°
   y = 130°
4. x = 40°
   y = 110°
5. a = 145°
   b = 100°
6. c = 75°
   d = 120°
7. r = 60°
   s = 120°
8. n = 105°
   y = 70°
9. x = 40°
   y = 20°
10. b = 30°
    c = 140°
11. a = 55°
    b = 125°
12. m = 35°
    n = 65°

Page 13
1. square
2. triangle
3. parallelogram
4. rhombus
5. pentagon
6. hexagon
7. rhombus
8. octagon
9. rectangle
10. trapezoid
11. triangle
12. square

Page 14
1. 110°
2. 100°
3. 100°
7. 90°
8. 60°
9. 100°

4. 130°
5. 90°
6. 40°
10. 130°
11. 120°
12. 55°

Page 15
1. 64 m
2. 78 ft.
3. 76 cm
4. 150 in.
5. 110 yd.
6. 164 mm
7. 342 cm
8. 468 mm
9. 533 m
10. 438 in.
11. 53.2 m
12. 109.76 cm

Page 16
1. 130 yds.
2. 260 cm
3. 330 ft.
4. 630 m
5. 250 cm
6. 722 mm
7. 221 m
8. 85.8 cm

Page 17
1. 80 m
2. 150 cm
3. 124 yds.
4. 105 mm
5. 180 in.
6. 75 mm
7. 92 ft.
8. 114 cm
9. 194 m
10. 323 mm

Page 18
1. 31.4 in.
2. 37.68 m
3. 28.26 in.
4. 25.12 ft.
5. 47.1 cm
6. 62.8 m
7. 78.5 ft.
8. 94.2 in.

Page 19
1. 31.4 ft.
2. 125.6 cm
3. 43.96 ft.
4. 69.08 in.
5. 25.12 m
6. 47.1 cm
7. 113.04 ft.
8. 125.6 yd.
9. 100.48 m
10. 502.4 mm

Page 20
1. 12 cm²
2. 12 cm²
3. 18 cm²
4. 22 cm²
5. 30 cm²
6. 9 cm²
7. 9 cm²
8. 27 cm²
9. 20 cm²
10. 33 cm²

Page 21
1. 600 in.²
2. 300 m²
3. 414 cm²
4. 2,961 mm²
5. 1,425 ft.²
6. 5,103 m²
7. 5,472 yards²
8. 2,204 in.²
9. 5,896 m²
10. 3,619 cm²
11. 26.27 m²
12. 119.31 ft.²
13. 9.87 in.²
14. 36.48 cm²

Page 22
1. 750 m²
2. 1,000 mm²
3. 1,386 ft.²
4. 4,920 in.²
5. 2,324 in.²
6. 31.5 m²
7. 2,296 mm²
8. 24.8 ft.²
9. 14,400 in.²
10. 38 m²
11. 4,840 mm²
12. 23.25 in.²
13. 19.84 m²
14. 61,200 cm²

Page 23
1. 2,700 cm²
2. 3,150 m²
3. 2,970 in.²
4. 6,740 m²
5. 10,800 ft.²
6. 37.8 cm²
7. 120,000 ft.²
8. 10.29 m²
9. 89,298 cm²
10. 44.16 in.²
11. 4,410 m²
12. 280,200 mm²
13. 356,000 in.²
14. 89,284 m²

Answer Key (cont.)

Page 24
1. 120 in.²
2. 270 m²
3. 660 ft.²
4. 377 mm²
5. 1,175 cm²
6. 3,735 mm²
7. 1,138.5 in.²
8. 60,000 cm²

Page 25
1. 180 mm²
2. 680 ft.²
3. 440 in.²
4. 792 m²
5. 1,680 cm²
6. 475 ft.²
7. 638 yards²
8. 14.08 cm²

Page 26
1. 78.5 in.²
2. 28.26 m²
3. 254.34 yards²
4. 452.16 cm²
5. 113.04 ft.²
6. 379.94 m²
7. 314 in.²
8. 5,024 cm²

Page 27
1. 200.96 in.²
2. 706.5 cm²
3. 2,826 ft.²
4. 7,850 mm²
5. 1,256 in.²
6. 530.66 m²

Page 28
1. 125 cm³
2. 1,728 in.³
3. 8,000 ft.³
4. 729 mm³
5. 1,331 yards³
6. 1,000 cm³
7. 27,000 mm³
8. 0.216 yards³

Page 29
1. 400 cm³
2. 1,080 m³
3. 1,800 in.³
4. 3,600 ft.³
5. 5,400 yards³
6. 1,800 cm³
7. 11 ft.³
8. 5.4 m³

Page 30
1. 1,320 mm³
2. 2,520 ft.³
3. 6,250 m³
4. 30,000 cm³

5. 36,960 in.³
6. 5,400 mm³
7. 47.25 m³
8. 32.55 cm³

Page 31
1. 24 in.³
2. 48 ft.³
3. 80 mm³
4. 40 in.³
5. 200 in.³
6. 150 cm³
7. 210 m³
8. 346.7 ft.³

Page 32
1. 549.5 cm³
2. 502.4 in.³
3. 2,009.6 ft.³
4. 10,173.6 cm.³
5. 1,205.76 in.³
6. 1,130.4 m³
7. 1,692.46 mm³
8. 602.88 cm³

Page 33
1. *face 1:* 32 m
   face 2: 32 m
   face 3: 40 m
   face 4: 40 m
   face 5: 80 m
   face 6: 80 m
   total 304 m²
2. *face 1:* 35 ft.
   face 2: 35 ft.
   face 3: 20 ft.
   face 4: 20 ft.
   face 5: 28 ft.
   face 6: 28 ft.
   total 166 ft.²
3. *face 1:* 110 cm
   face 2: 110 cm
   face 3: 55 cm
   face 4: 55 cm
   face 5: 50 cm
   face 6: 50 cm
   total 430 cm²
4. *face 1:* 63 mm
   face 2: 63 mm
   face 3: 70 mm
   face 4: 70 mm
   face 5: 90 mm
   face 6: 90 mm
   total 446 mm³
5. *face 1:* 200 in.
   face 2: 200 in.
   face 3: 220 in.
   face 4: 220 in.
   face 5: 110 in.
   face 6: 110 in.
   total 1,060 in.²

6. *face 1:* 120 m
   face 2: 120 m
   face 3: 108 m
   face 4: 108 m
   face 5: 90 m
   face 6: 90 m
   total 636 m²

Page 34

Page 35
Number 5 does not express rotational symmetry. All other shapes do.

Page 36
1. A, B, D
2. A, B, C
3. B, C
4. B, D and A, C
5. A, D
6. A and C, B and D

Page 37
1. Similar – A, C, D
   Congruent – A, D
2. Similar – B, C, D
   Congruent – B, C
3. Similar – A, B, C, D
   Congruent – B, D
4. Similar – A, B, C
   Congruent – A, C
5. Similar – B, D
   Congruent – A, B
6. Similar – A, B; C, D
   Congruent – A, D

Page 38
1. cylinder
2. triangular pyramid
3. square pyramid
4. sphere
5. dodecahedron
6. cone
7. octahedron
8. cube
9. rectangular prism
10. triangular pyramid/tetrahedron
11. icosahedron
12. triangular prism

Page 39
1. rectangular prism
   F = 6
   E = 12
   V = 8
2. square pyramid
   F = 5
   E = 8
   V = 5
3. tetrahedron/triangular pyramid
   F = 4
   E = 6
   V = 4
4. cube
   F = 6
   E = 12
   V = 8
5. octahedron
   F = 8
   E = 12
   V = 6
6. dodecahedron
   F = 12
   E = 30
   V = 20
7. triangular prism
   F = 5
   E = 9
   V = 6
8. icosahedron
   F = 20
   E = 30
   V = 12

Page 40
1. A
2. B
3. A
4. D
5. A
6. B
7. B
8. B
9. A
10. A
11. D
12. A
13. B
14. B

Page 41
1. A
2. A
3. A
4. C
5. C
6. B
7. A
8. B
9. C
10. C
11. D
12. B

Page 42
1. C
2. C
3. B
4. D
5. C
6. A
7. A
8. B
9. D
10. A

Page 43
1. B
2. D
3. C
4. B
5. D
6. A
7. D
8. A
9. C
10. D

Page 44
1. B
2. C
3. D
4. C
5. C
6. A
7. A
8. A
9. C
10. B

Page 45
1. D
2. A
3. A
4. B
5. B
6. D
7. D
8. C
9. D
10. B

#8626 *Practice Makes Perfect: Geometry*   © *Teacher Created Resources, Inc.*